Kid's Keyboard Kingdom

Katherine Galloway

AuthorHouse™ LLC
1663 Liberty Drive
Bloomington, IN 47403
www.authorhouse.com
Phone: 1-800-839-8640

Published by AuthorHouse: 11/21/2013

ISBN: 978-1-4918-8192-7 (sc)
ISBN: 978-1-4918-8202-3 (e)

authorHOUSE®

Preface

This book has been designed for the very young keyboard player (approximately age 5+), not as a tutor book but as a supplement. The ideas have been developed to help children in the very early stages of music tuition read notes in treble clef and play in various positions with the right hand. The book is set out in a visually attractive way to inspire the imagination of young children. Rhythm has deliberately been separated from the notation to help the very young child focus on one aspect of note reading.

In colouring the notes, the child is not only developing their reading of the musical notation on the musical staff, but also developing their hand-eye coordination, an essential skill for playing any musical instrument.

With the help of a skilled teacher/adult, rhythm could be introduced for example, clapping rhythms to copy or adding the backing accompaniment to the keyboard and playing on the beat.

All these ideas have been thoroughly enjoyed by many pupils of mine and have been a very good stepping stone to reading and understanding musical notation. The keyboard seems to be an increasingly popular and accessible instrument to many young children that such a book should help enthuse an interest in reading and playing music from an early age.

Table of Contents

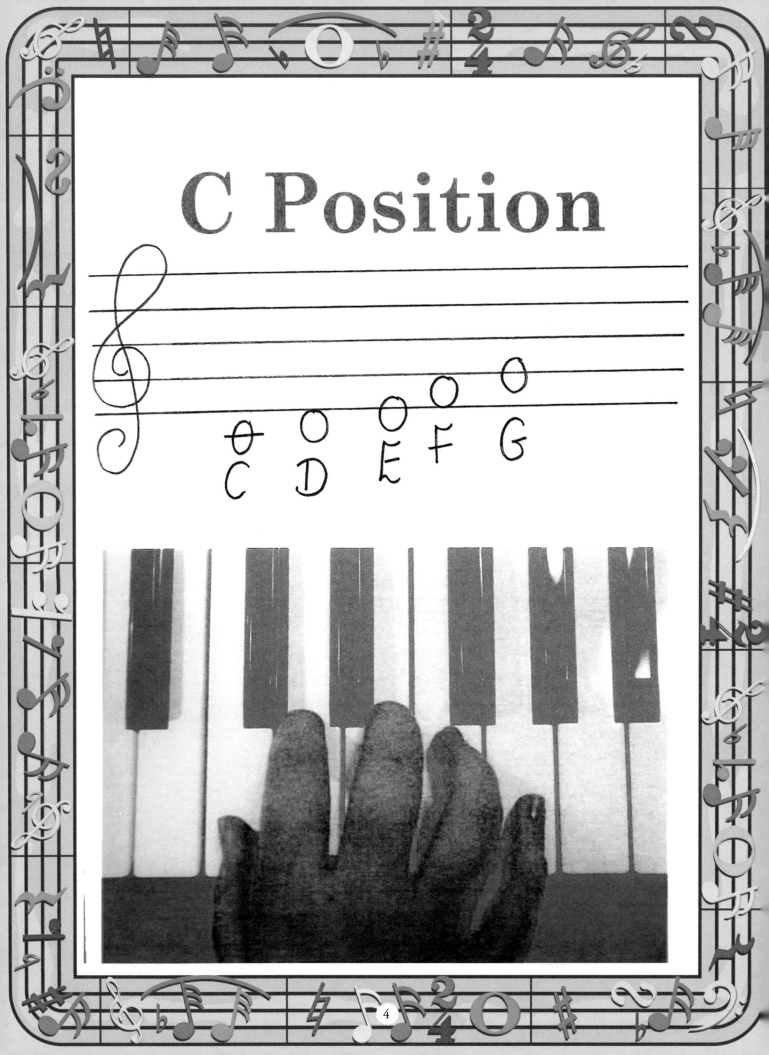

BUSY TRAFFIC

Colour and play:
C's...yellow
D's...purple
E's...orange
F's...pink
G's...blue

Can you make the music sound like busy traffic by playing fast?

Tea time.

Colour and play:
C's.....red
D's.....yellow
E's.....purple
F's.....pink
G's.....green

Dinosoar Prints.

Colour and play:
C's.....red
D's.....yellow
E's.....blue
F's.....orange
G's.....green

Hen and her chicks.

Colour and play:

C's.....red
D's.....yellow
E's.....green
F's.....blue
G's.....orange

Juggling Clown.

Colour and Play:
C's.....red
D's.....blue
E's.....yellow
F's.....orange
G's.....purple

Singing Birds.

Colour and play:
C's.....yellow
D's.....blue
E's.....pink
F's.....orange
G's.....purple

swinging elephant trunk.

Colour and play:
C's......yellow
D's......orange
E's......purple
F's......pink
G's......green

Cat Prints.

mi ~ ow!

Colour and play:
C's.....yellow
D's.....red
E's.....blue
F's.....orange
G's.....green

Dancing Ducks!

Colour and Play:

D's...red

E's...green

F's...

G's...orange

A's...blue

Warm woolly sheep.

Colour and play:
D's.....red
E's.....pink
F's.....orange
G's.....green
A's.....yellow

Swinging Monkey.

Colour and play:
D's......yellow
E's......purple
F's......blue
G's......green
A's......orange

Over the rainbow.

Colour and play:
D's.....blue
E's.....red
F's.....purple
G's.....green
A's.....orange

Little yummy mouse nibbles.

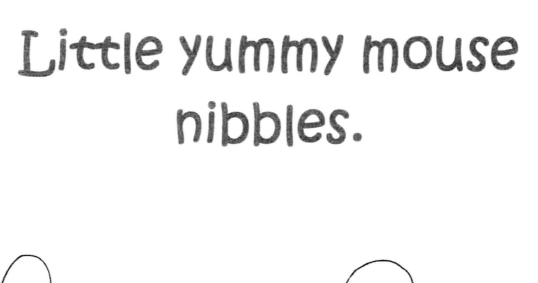

Colour and play:
D's.....red
E's.....orange
F's.....yellow
G's.....green
A's.....purple

Tribute to 'Bach'!

Colour and play:
D's......red
E's......blue
F's......orange
G's......green
A's......yellow

Spot the ladybird trail.

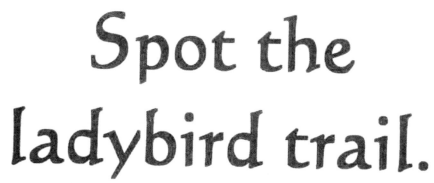

Colour and play:
D's......yellow
E's......red
F's......orange
G's......purple
A's......green.

E Position

A brewing tune!

Colour and play:
E's.....orange
F's.....yellow
G's.....green
A's.....red
B's.....blue

A Flowering Song!

Colour and Play:

E's...red

F's...pink

G's...

A's...orange

B's...blue

A fruity tune.

Colour and play:
E's.....red
F's.....purple
G's.....orange
A's.....yellow
B's.....green

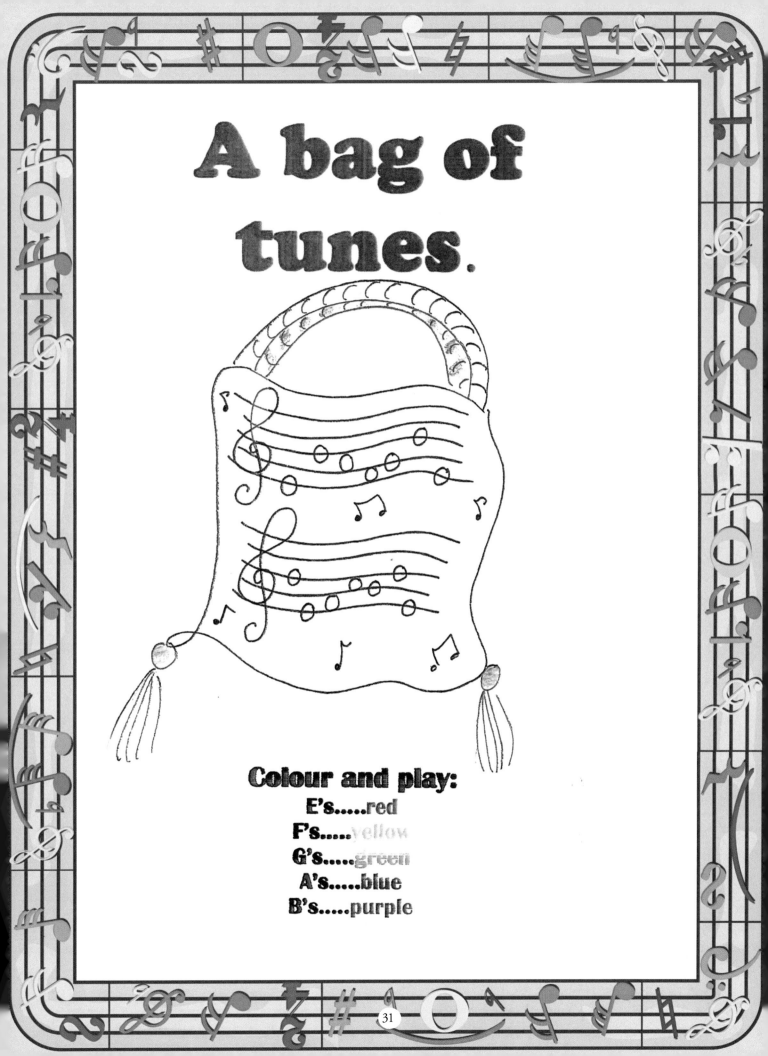

A bag of tunes.

Colour and play:
E's.....red
F's.....yellow
G's.....green
A's.....blue
B's.....purple

A little buzzing tune.

Colour and play:
E's.....orange
F's.....yellow
G's.....green
A's.....red
B's.....blue

The flying pig.

Colour and play:
F's......red
G's......orange
A's......yellow
B's......blue
C's......green

Swinging apples.

Colour and play:
F's.....yellow
G's.....orange
A's.....purple
B's.....blue
C's.....pink

A fizzy pop tune.

Colour and play:
F's.....yellow
G's.....green
A's.....red
B's.....blue
C's.....pink

Flying high.

Colour and play:
F's.....yellow
G's.....green
A's.....orange
B's.....blue
C's.....purple

The singing moon.

Colour and play:

F's...red
G's...green
A's...orange
B's...blue
C's...yellow

....and a word from 'Mr.Moon'..."keep practising and reach for the stars"!

Spotty singing cow.

Colour and play:
F's.....blue
G's.....green
A's.....yellow
B's.....orange
C's.....purple

A red hot tune.

Colour and play:

F's......red

G's......orange

A's......green

B's......blue

C's......yellow

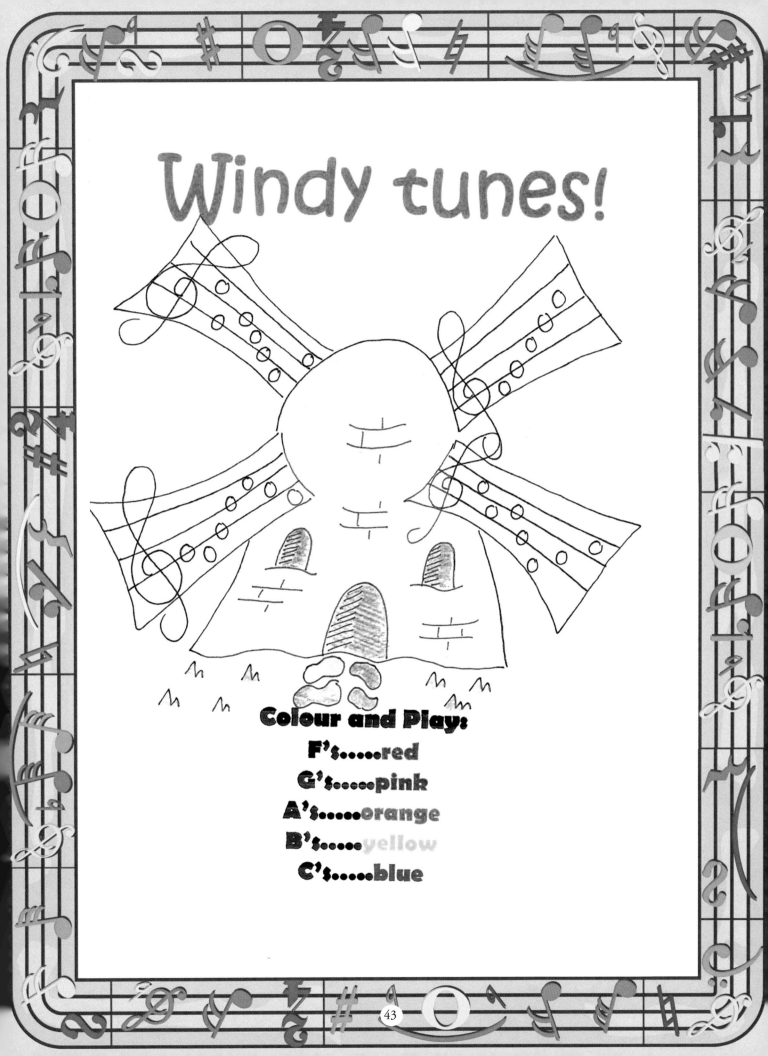

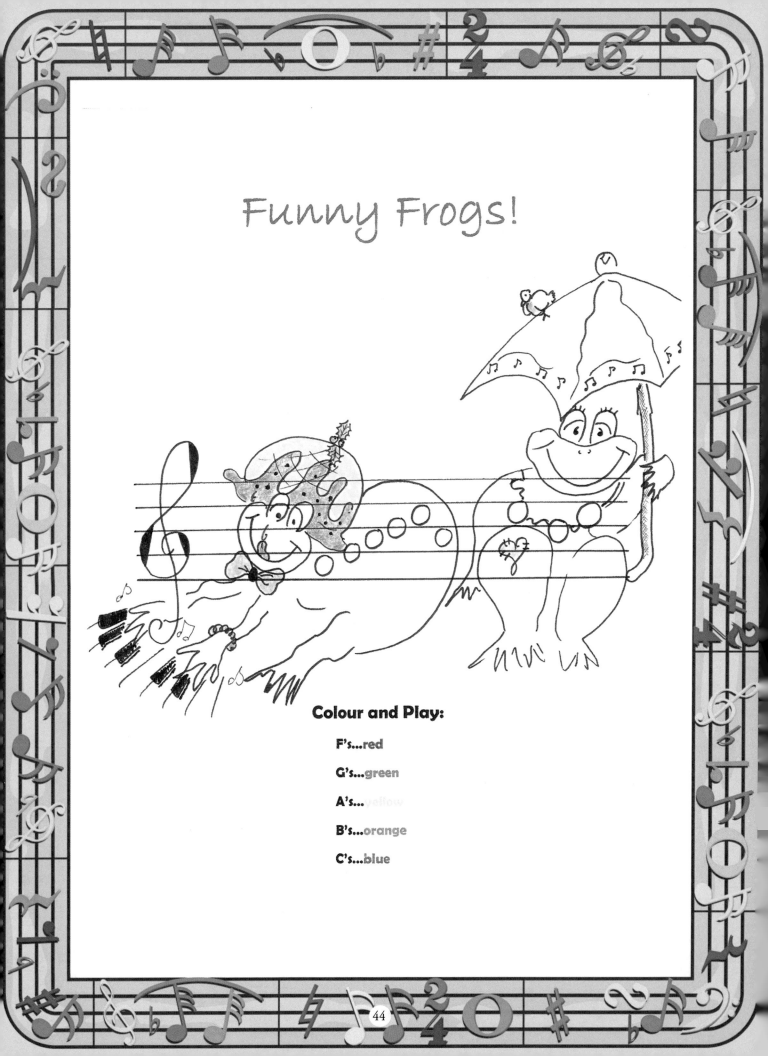

Funny Frogs!

Colour and Play:

F's...red

G's...green

A's...yellow

B's...orange

C's...blue

G Position

G A B C D

A little tune ringing in your ears.

Colour and play:
G's......green
A's......red
B's......blue
C's......yellow
D's......orange

Yummy icecream

Colour and play:
G's.....green
A's.....yellow
B's.....blue
C's.....orange
D's.....pink

The Singing Starfish!

Colour and play:
G's.....pink
A's.....blue
B's.....orange
C's.....yellow
D's.....green

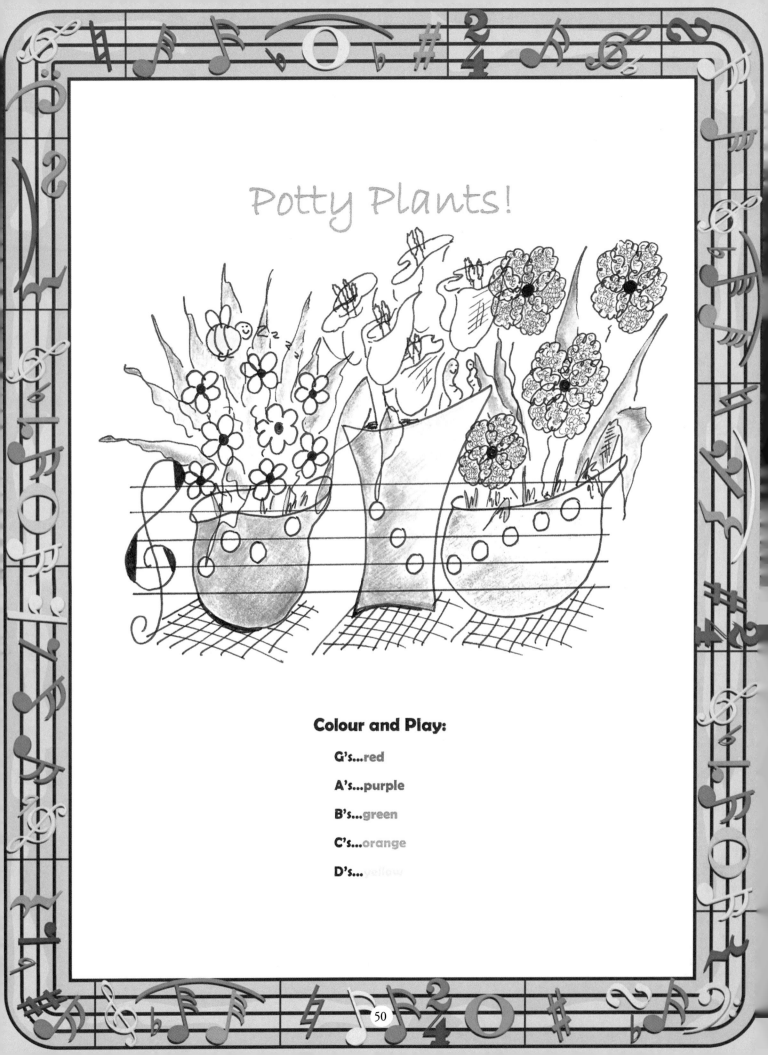

Potty Plants!

Colour and Play:

G's...red

A's...purple

B's...green

C's...orange

D's...yellow

Tuneful toadstool!

Colour and play:
G's......red
A's......yellow
B's......blue
C's......green
D's......orange

Flying Kites!

Colour and Play:

G's...red

A's...pink

B's...yellow

C's...orange

D's...blue

Tootling tortoise!

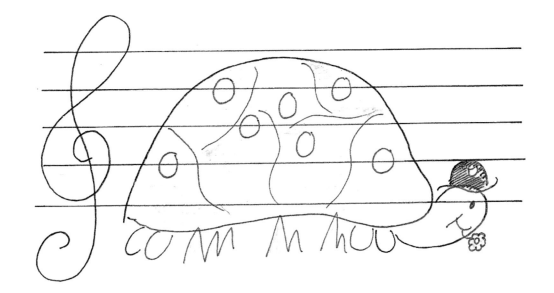

Colour and play:
G's.....red
A's.....yellow
B's.....blue
C's.....orange
D's.....pink

Ship A-hoy!

Colour and play:
G's.....yellow
A's.....blue
B's.....red
C's.....green
D's.....orange

A bucketful of tunes!

Colour and play:

G's......green
A's......yellow
B's......pink
C's......blue
D's......orange

B Position

Boogie Dancing Bananas!

Colour and play:

B's.....yellow

C's.....purple

D's......red

E's.....orange

F's.....green

A jammy tune!

Colour and play:
B's.....red
C's.....orange
D's.....
E's.....blue
F's.....pink

Colour and play:

B's......orange

C's......

D's......blue

E's......pink

F's......green

A balloonful of tunes!

Colour and play:
B's......yellow
C's......orange
D's......blue
E's......red
F's......green

A bouncy tune.

Colour and play:
B's.....blue
C's.....
 D's.....pink
E's.....purple
F's.....orange

The singing bookworm!

Colour and play:
B's.....blue
C's.....
D's.....red
E's.....orange
F's.....pink

A short
snappy tune.

Colour and play:
B's.....
C's.....red
D's.....green
E's.....blue
F's.....orange

Birthday cake.

Colour and play:
- B's.....blue
- C's.....
- D's.....pink
- E's.....orange
- F's.....purple

A cracking good tune!

Colour and play:
B's......red
C's......pink
D's......blue
E's.....
F's...... orange

69

A roaring tune!

Colour and play:
B's......red
C's......yellow
D's......blue
E's......orange
F's......green

A little bear song

Colour and play:
B's.....blue
C's.....red
D's.....
E's.....purple
F's.....orange

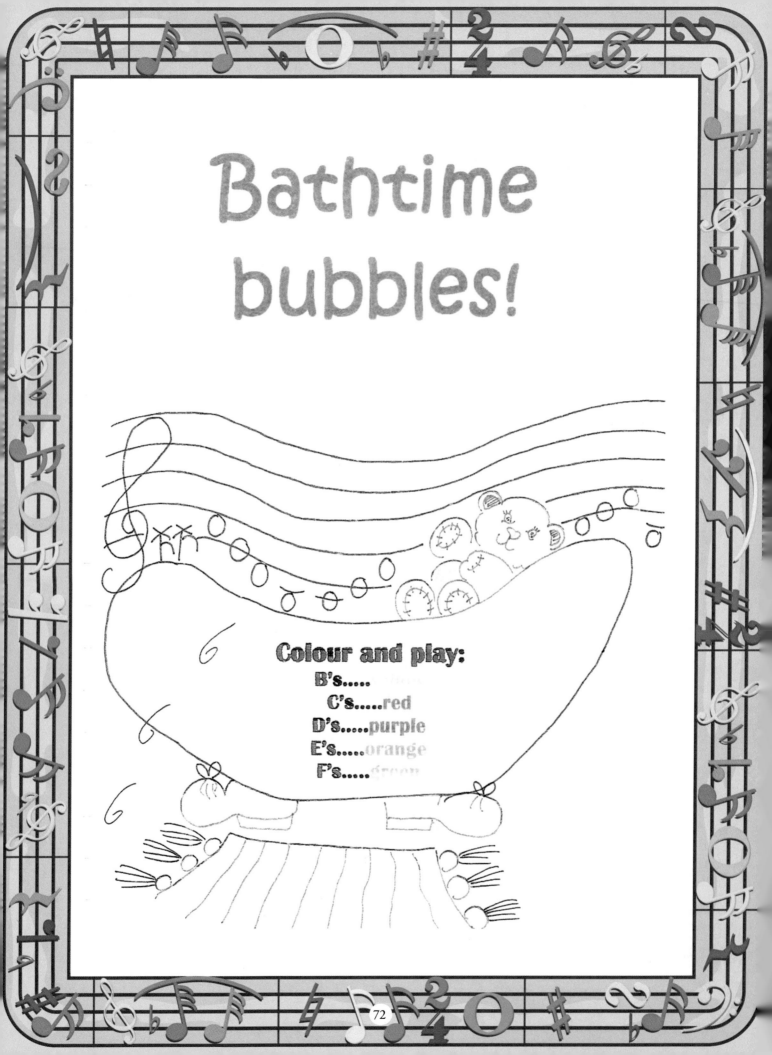

A Position

A   B   C   D   E

Kangaroo Hops!

Colour and play:

A's......orange
B's......yellow
C's......green
D's......pink
E's......purple

Singing Seal!

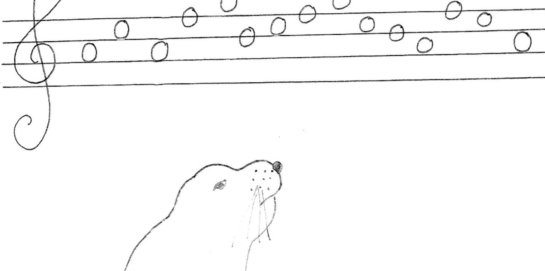

Colour and play:

A's......purple

B's......orange

C's......red

D's......green

E's......blue

SMART PENGUIN PARDE!

Colour and play:
A's......blue
B's......red
C's......pink
D's......green
E's......orange

Diggin' for a little tune!

Colour and play:

A's......blue

B's......orange

C's......

D's......green

E's......red

Whistle as you write!

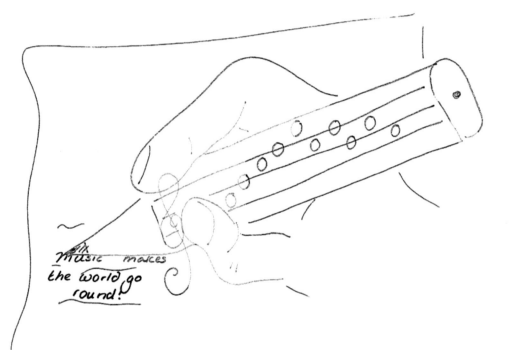

Colour and play:

A's..........red

B's..........orange

C's..........yellow

D's..........green

E's..........blue

The Song of Saturn!

Colour and play:
A's......red
B's......blue
C's......green
D's......pink
E's......orange

A Ruggy Ragtime Songs!

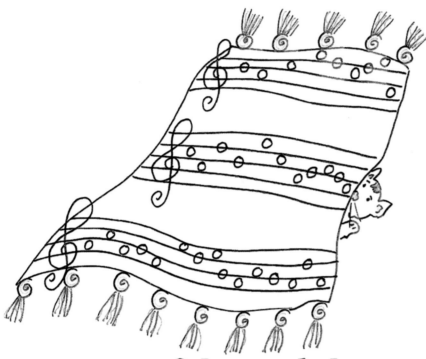

Colour and play:
A's......red
B's......orange
C's......yellow
D's......green
E's......blue

Yummy Cherry Buns!

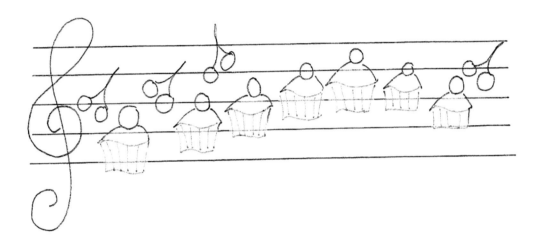

Colour and play:

A's......red

B's......green

C's......blue

D's......orange

E's......

Bunny's Beads!

Colour and play:
A's......orange
B's......yellow
C's......green
D's......blue
E's......red

Colour and play:

A's.....

B's.....purple

C's.....red

D's.....

E's.....green

Sing for your Supper!

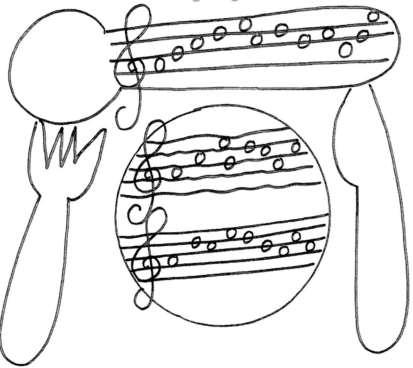

Colour and play:
A's......red
B's......orange
C's......pink
D's......blue
E's......yellow

Printed in the United States
By Bookmasters